Big Panda
and
Tiny Dragon

Big Panda
and
Tiny Dragon

James Norbury

MANDALA

SAN RAFAEL LOS ANGELES LONDON

This book is dedicated
to everyone who gets lost.

Contents

Spring	6
Summer	46
Autumn	78
Winter	122
Spring	148
Afterword	157

Spring

Be brave.

You never know what a
first meeting might lead to.

8 spring

"A new day and a new beginning,"
said Tiny Dragon.

"What shall we do with it?"

"Which is more important," asked Big Panda, "the journey or the destination?"

"The company," said Tiny Dragon.

"I'm too busy to see the flowers right now," said Tiny Dragon.

"All the more reason to look at them," said Big Panda. "And they might not be here tomorrow."

"Isn't nature incredible!" said Tiny Dragon.

"It is," agreed Big Panda.
"But we are just as much a part of nature
as the tree or the spider, and just as amazing."

"Big Panda," said Tiny Dragon,
"I like the way you listen to me
and talk to me and travel with me,
but most of all, I like the way
you make me feel."

"Try to make time for the small things,"
said Big Panda. "They are often the most important."

"The most important thing . . ."
said Big Panda, ". . . is to pay attention."

"Just because you don't know where you are going, it doesn't mean you are lost," said Tiny Dragon profoundly.

"Very true," replied Big Panda. "But in this case we are definitely lost."

"That tree has been through some rough times,"
said Tiny Dragon.

"Yes," said Big Panda, "but it's still here,
and it has gained strength and beauty."

"Hurry!" squeaked Tiny Dragon.
"There is so much to do!"

"The river doesn't hurry," said Big Panda,
"yet despite many obstacles,
it always gets where it's going."

"Nothing is happening," said Tiny Dragon.

"Maybe," said Big Panda,
"it's happening underneath first."

"Sometimes I think I'm not good enough," said Tiny Dragon.

"A cherry tree doesn't compare itself to other trees," said Big Panda. "It just blossoms."

Uses for a leaf: no. 1—a boat.

Sometimes, you just have to be silly.

spring 35

Each decision you make on your journey takes you closer or further from where you want to go.

"Mistakes mean you're trying," said Big Panda.
"Don't give up."

"I want to change the world," said Tiny Dragon.

"Start with the next person who needs your help," replied Big Panda.

"The map doesn't show
where I'm supposed to go,"
said Tiny Dragon.

"Your journey isn't shown
on any map," said Big Panda.
"You must discover your own path."

"I miss him already," said Tiny Dragon.
"What if he gets hurt?"

"You helped him when he needed it most,"
said Big Panda.
"And what if he goes on to live a long
and happy life?"

"The path ahead looks difficult," said Big Panda.

"No matter how hard it gets," said Tiny Dragon, "we'll face it together."

"I wish this moment could last forever,"
said Tiny Dragon.

"This moment is all there is,"
said Big Panda.

Summer

Time doing nothing is never wasted.

"I wish I had met you earlier,"
said Tiny Dragon, "so we could have gone
on even more adventures together."

"What is my purpose?" asked Tiny Dragon.

Big Panda paused, then said,
"To sit on that stone and be with your friend."

"My head feels like this storm sometimes,"
said Tiny Dragon.

"If you really listen," said Big Panda,
"you can hear the raindrops
splashing on the stone.
It's possible to find a little peace,
even in a storm."

An Elder Dragon
is a Tiny Dragon
who never gave up.

"We have a long way to go," said Big Panda.

Tiny Dragon grinned. "Grandpa Dragon used to say, 'A journey of a thousand miles begins with a cup of tea.'"

"You're a good listener," said Tiny Dragon.

"Listening has never landed me in trouble," replied Big Panda.

"I can't find the right place for this last branch," huffed Tiny Dragon.

Big Panda chewed his bamboo thoughtfully. "It's the imperfections that make it perfect."

"The best thing to have with tea,"
said Big Panda, "is a good friend."

"I'm worried," said Tiny Dragon.
"I don't know what to do next."

"For just a moment," said Big Panda,
"stop, breathe, and listen to
the wind in the bamboo."

"What are you doing?"
asked Tiny Dragon.

"I've no idea," said Big Panda,
"but it's great fun."

If you seek happiness for others,
you may find it for yourself.

"You know," said Tiny Dragon, "these might be the good old days that we'll look back on with great longing."

"In that case," said Big Panda, "let's never stop making memories."

Love needs no explanation.

Together, we can do anything.

Some people are like candles.

They burn themselves out
to create light for others.

Uses for a leaf: no. 17—a parasol (and dinner).

"Hurry up, Big Panda,
we're going to be late!"

Big Panda sat down.
"I like to think I'm creating anticipation."

"This garden is beautiful," said Tiny Dragon.

Big Panda nodded. "And we only found it because we went the wrong way so many times."

summer 75

"You don't do much,"
said Tiny Dragon.

"I'm full of potential,"
said Big Panda with a yawn.

Autumn

"Autumn is here," said Big Panda,
"and soon winter will be upon us."

"Ooh . . ." said Tiny Dragon.
"More cozy evenings together . . . with tea."

Uses for a leaf: no. 62—an umbrella.

"We're lost again," said Big Panda.

"When I'm lost," said Tiny Dragon, "I find it helps to go back to the beginning and try to remember why I started."

"What if I meet people who don't like me or the things I do?" asked Tiny Dragon.

"You must walk your own path," said Big Panda. "Better to lose them than lose yourself."

"My flower . . ." said Tiny Dragon.

"All things must come to pass, little one.
That's what makes them so precious."

"It's hard being kind to everyone," said Tiny Dragon.

"True," said Big Panda, "and hardest of all to be kind to ourselves, but we must try."

Let go or be dragged.

When drinking tea . . . drink tea.

"What are you thinking about?"
asked Tiny Dragon.

"Nothing," said Big Panda.
"It's wonderful."

"I can't find my way out of this hole,"
said Tiny Dragon.

Big Panda smiled.
"Then I will come and sit in it with you."

"The leaves are dying," said Tiny Dragon.

"Don't be sad," said Big Panda. "Autumn is nature's way of showing us how beautiful letting go can be."

autumn 97

"Look what I found," said Tiny Dragon.

"Oh," said Big Panda,
"an opportunity to try something new."

"You're quiet today," said Tiny Dragon.

Big Panda smiled. "I don't think I can improve on the sound of the rain."

"I'm not sure this is working . . ."

"How is that tree still standing?" asked Tiny Dragon.

"During better times," said Big Panda, "it grew deep roots. Now it can weather any storm."

"It's a shame we didn't plant this tree a long time ago," said Tiny Dragon. "Imagine how big it would be."

"We're doing it now," said Big Panda.
"That's the important thing."

"Can you hear the wind in the trees, Tiny Dragon?
That's nature's way of telling us to take a moment
to stop, breathe, and just be."

"Are you ever mean to yourself, Big Panda?"

Big Panda watched the ripples spread across the lake.

"I see how gentle you are, Tiny Dragon,
and try to treat myself with the same kindness."

"There have been so many difficulties along this path," said Tiny Dragon.

"There have," agreed Big Panda, "but we have learned something from each one. And imagine how good the view will be when we reach the top."

"Whether people praise you
or criticize you, Tiny Dragon,
try to accept it gracefully.
It takes all kinds of conditions to
create a strong tree."

Listening to someone is one of the
greatest things you can do for them.

110 autumn

When you light a lantern
for someone else,
you cannot help but
light up your own path.

"If you don't try," said Big Panda,
"you'll never know if you can fly."

"I'm tired," sighed Tiny Dragon.

"Then it's time to stop," said Big Panda. "Watch the stars, and have a cup of hot tea."

"What are you celebrating?" asked Tiny Dragon.

"Getting rained on," said Big Panda. "With you."

"That's a very small candle," said Tiny Dragon.

"However small the light," said Big Panda, "it's better than darkness."

"I want to open a scary pumpkin stand," said Tiny Dragon, "but I'm afraid I'll fail."

Big Panda poured his friend some more tea.

"You might fail, little one, but if you let fear stop you from even trying, failure is assured."

Sometimes all you can do
is make someone a cup of tea.

It might be enough.

There are days
when just getting up is a victory.

"What is the universe?" asked Tiny Dragon.

Big Panda looked up at the night sky.

"We are, little one. We are depthless oceans and summer lightning—there is nothing more magnificent."

autumn 121

Winter

"You've been carrying me for so many days now,"
said Tiny Dragon.

"It could be worse," said Big Panda.
"We could be Big Dragon and Tiny Panda."

"Each season is completely different," said Big Panda, "yet each has its wonders."

"Just like us," said Tiny Dragon with a grin.

Sometimes, it's good to head out
with no idea where you're going.

"How do you keep going?"
asked Tiny Dragon.

"Sometimes," said Big Panda,
"even the smallest step
is better than no step."

"It's the shortest day," said Tiny Dragon. "Winter is truly upon us."

"But also the longest night," said Big Panda, "and that comes with its own wonders."

"I give up," said Tiny Dragon.

"That's OK," said Big Panda.
"We'll try again tomorrow."

"It's cold and dark tonight," said Tiny Dragon.

"Don't worry, little one," said Big Panda.
"The sun will rise again."

"If you're struggling, little one, you can tell me," said Big Panda.
"I want to help."

"Do bad thoughts make me a bad person?" asked Tiny Dragon.

"No," said Big Panda. "The waves are not the ocean. The thoughts are not the mind."

"I am so tired," said Tiny Dragon.

Big Panda paused. "Winter is a time when nature withdraws, rests, and gathers its energy for a new beginning. We are allowed to do the same, my little friend."

winter 135

"I forgot to make my New Year's resolution," sighed Tiny Dragon.

"Don't worry, little one," said Big Panda. "If there's something you want to change, you can start right now."

"What would your three wishes be?"
asked Tiny Dragon.

Big Panda pondered a moment.
"Us together . . . traveling . . . in the rain."

"There is beauty everywhere," said Big Panda,
"but sometimes it's difficult to see."

Uses for a leaf: no. 111—a sled.

"I can't explain how I feel,"
said Tiny Dragon.

Big Panda smiled. "That's OK.
Words are not adequate for all things."

"You give me strength when all mine has gone."

Spring

Butterflies struggle most just before they emerge.

"Do you believe in reincarnation?"
asked Tiny Dragon.

Big Panda yawned. "I believe that
every minute of every day,
we can let go and start again."

Even a damaged tree can produce
the most beautiful blossoms.

"Are we nearly there yet?"
asked Tiny Dragon.

Big Panda smiled.
"I hope not."

Afterword

Some time ago, while I was in a difficult place, I happened across a book on Buddhism in a second-hand bookshop. I found the content fascinating and began investigating spirituality and meditation in greater depth. The more I learned, the more I realized I didn't need to be a slave to my negative thoughts.

Having discovered something that so improved my happiness, I became more determined to help others. I joined the Samaritans, taking calls from people reaching out for help with loneliness, anxiety, and depression. The amount of human suffering really shocked me and inspired me to start a small support group for my local area, but the arrival of COVID-19 put a stop to those plans.

Instead, I decided to draw pictures as a way of communicating these powerful, transformational ideas to people in simple, accessible ways. Initially, I had no idea how successful it would be, but I've been contacted by people from many different cultures, religions, countries, and age groups, letting me know how much my pictures have helped them through difficult times.

I put all my heart into each picture, and I think that's why they speak to people—each and every one has a little piece of my soul in it.

Acknowledgments

This book is the culmination of a lifetime's experience. I therefore acknowledge everyone I've ever met; you have all forged me into the person I am now, and if I were not that person, I could not have created this—so thank you.

But some people really stand out as having made this book a reality.

Ruth, who has always helped me just by being herself. She's the center of my world, and I love her more each day.

My mother and father, who taught me to be self-reliant, to value art as a way to convey ideas, and who supported me with all my strange plans. Without them in my life, I would have never believed it possible to make a living from art—thank you.

My brother and sister, Alan and Jayne—you're always so encouraging and supporting.

Ludo, I can't believe you did it. I wrote to so many agents, and you are the only one who believed in me. Thank you so much. I hope your faith is rewarded. I like to think I have gained a friend and an agent. And Eve, I know how much you do behind the scenes—thank you.

Dan, I really lucked out with you. I could not imagine any other editor having shared my vision so strongly or understood so deeply what I was trying to do. And many thanks to everyone else at Penguin Books UK who has worked so hard to bring my funny little pictures to the world—Aggie, Bea, Sarah, Lee, Jon, Tracy, Dan P-B, Rebecca, Anjali, Vanessa, Sophie, Ellie, and Christina.

My followers on social media, without your support and encouragement I would not have carried on. Thank you.

My fellow Samaritans, it can be rough sometimes; knowing we are all there for each other makes a huge difference. Talking on the phone with the callers is a privilege, and their words have changed me in ways I can't explain. I don't think this book would exist without them.

And of course, my animal friends—you keep me sane while driving me insane.

MANDALA

An Imprint of MandalaEarth
PO Box 3088
San Rafael, CA 94912
www.MandalaEarth.com

Find us on Facebook: www.facebook.com/MandalaEarth
Follow us on Twitter: @MandalaEarth

First published in Great Britain by Michael Joseph
Text copyright © James Norbury 2021
Illustration copyright © James Norbury 2021
The author has asserted his moral rights

All rights reserved. Published by Mandala Publishing in 2021.
No part of this book may be reproduced in any form without written permission from the publisher.

Library of Congress Cataloging-in-Publication Data available.

ISBN: 978-1-64722-512-4

Slipcase Gift Set ISBN: 979-8-88762-019-0

CEO: Raoul Goff
Publisher: Roger Shaw
VP of Manufacturing: Alix Nicholaeff
Art Director: Ashley Quackenbush
Editorial Director: Katie Killebrew
Editorial Assistant: Amanda Nelson
Senior Production Manager: Joshua Smith
Senior Production Manager, Subsidiary Rights: Lina s Palma-Temena

Mandala Publishing, in association with Roots of Peace, will plant two trees for each tree used in the manufacturing of this book. Roots of Peace is an internationally renowned humanitarian organization dedicated to eradicating land mines worldwide and converting war-torn lands into productive farms and wildlife habitats. Roots of Peace will plant two million fruit and nut trees in Afghanistan and provide farmers there with the skills and support necessary for sustainable land use.

Manufactured in China by Insight Editions

10 9 8 7 6 5 4 3

MANDALA

An Imprint of MandalaEarth
PO Box 3088
San Rafael, CA 94912
www.MandalaEarth.com

Find us on Facebook: www.facebook.com/MandalaEarth
Follow us on Twitter: @MandalaEarth

First published in Great Britain by Michael Joseph
Text © 2022 James Norbury
Illustrations © 2022 James Norbury
The author has asserted his moral rights

All rights reserved. Published by Mandala Publishing in 2023.
No part of this book may be reproduced in any form without written permission from the publisher.

ISBN: 978-1-64722-973-3

Slipcase Gift Set ISBN: 979-8-88762-019-0

CEO: Raoul Goff
Publisher: Roger Shaw
VP of Manufacturing: Alix Nicholaeff
Art Director: Ashley Quackenbush
Editorial Director: Katie Killebrew
Editorial Assistant: Amanda Nelson
Senior Production Manager: Joshua Smith
Senior Production Manager, Subsidiary Rights: Lina s Palma-Temena

Mandala Publishing, in association with Roots of Peace, will plant two trees for each tree used in the manufacturing of this book. Roots of Peace is an internationally renowned humanitarian organization dedicated to eradicating land mines worldwide and converting war-torn lands into productive farms and wildlife habitats. Roots of Peace will plant two million fruit and nut trees in Afghanistan and provide farmers there with the skills and support necessary for sustainable land use.

Manufactured in China by Insight Editions

10 9 8 7 6 5 4 3

Other aesthetic choices I have made include having the character generally move from left to right when things are progressing, and right to left when things are falling apart. I also changed to a completely different paint palette when the characters land in the new world to instill a subtle sense that everything is different.

I have also used, toward the front of the book, a Torii arch, which is a structure typically found on the way into Japanese Shinto temples and which represents the passage from the everyday material world into the more sacred, spiritual one.

It is my sincere hope that this story speaks to your heart and that if you find some of Tiny Dragon's struggle relatable, you might find some solace in the idea that change, albeit a little scary, is possible and with patience, can lead to better things.

The story essentially begins with change (Tiny Dragon's discontent) and ends with change (a new home in a new place). Both of these changes are scary, but both could be considered necessary to move through life and become less fearful and more content.

When I first set out to create the book, I decided to base it on the idea of a spiritual journey which starts not simply with discontent, but the acknowledgment of that discontent and the desire to do something about it. The protagonists then go on a journey of ups and downs – one minute things are looking up, then another disaster, then some light at the end of the tunnel, which is swiftly snuffed out. I feel personally this reflects my own experience and that of others I know, which I hope adds a bedrock of authenticity to the tale.

This led to a strange series of experiences where I often found myself so immersed in the process of expressing the character's emotional journey that my own feelings would begin to mirror those of Tiny Dragon and sometimes even Big Panda. Perhaps this is because their story is, in many ways, a retelling of my own.

I purposefully kept the book simple with only two characters. The scenery tends to mirror Tiny Dragon's mind state, where the bleaker he feels, the more barren the world becomes. I have endeavored to always make the world appear beautiful (because it is), but our little hero's perception of that world fluctuates, and I have tried to make the reader's experience mirror that.

Afterword

The Journey of *The Journey*

The original Big Panda and Tiny Dragon book was a compilation of individual drawings and dialogue that I created with the intent of sharing them on the internet. Although this created pictures which were very concise and immediate, they left me no way to explore a longer narrative.

In this second book, I have been able to tell a tale and that is one of the things I love the most.

I have always been attracted by the idea of a journey wherein the traveler struggles with both the environment and themselves. And although we tend to want our protagonist to succeed, I don't personally feel that success should be absolute. Life is not often like that and in a book like this I tried hard to avoid a happily-ever-after ending, thereby making it more relatable to the reader.

Yes, the characters do end up finding somewhere new to live and Tiny Dragon has discovered things about himself which will allow him to weather life's storm more easily, but they have both lost a great deal; they can never go home, they can never see their friends again and they are strangers in a strange land with all the fears and dangers that entails.

The End . . .

of this journey.

"There are so many unknowns and possibilities out there," said Tiny Dragon.

"Well then," said Big Panda, "let's see how many we can try."

That night Big Panda and Tiny Dragon slept deeply, their tired, aching bodies rested safely in the ruins of the old temple.

And as dawn broke across the mountains, they were greeted by the most magnificent sunrise heralding a new day and a new beginning.

"As long as we're alive," said Big Panda,
"we will keep making mistakes and end up getting lost;
that is the nature of things.

But as long as we're both here,
we'll keep helping each other and we will find our way."

Tiny Dragon poured his friend another cup of tea
and sat down next to him.

"Thank you," he said, stroking the big bear's head.

"What for?" asked Big Panda.

"I went wrong so many times, and every time you were there for me.
You never judged me, left me or scolded me.

I hope this time I've got it right."

Big Panda hugged the little dragon.

"I feel a bit like this cup," said Tiny Dragon.

"I've been through a tough time
and I feel like I've been damaged.

But these little cracks," he said,
holding the cup up to the moon,
"are what let the light shine through."

That night, they sat in the shadows of the ruined temple and drank tea made from spring water and fresh green buds.

"I don't think the world will ever be quite the way I want it to be," said Tiny Dragon, "and some things I can never change.

But I think maybe *I* have changed, so that those things that I couldn't accept before – I am starting to be OK with."

Then, just as they were thinking about stopping for the day, they saw what looked like a structure in the distance.

As they moved closer, they could see it was an ancient temple overgrown with trees and plants.

There were no signs of past occupants,
and aside from a few monkeys and birds,
no one seemed to pay them very much attention.

Big Panda checked inside and it seemed safe and sheltered.

"I think we may have found our new home."

"How are you so wise, Big Panda?"

Big Panda paused for a moment.

"We all have wisdom inside us, my little friend, but it's a very quiet, gentle voice, so you might need to be very still to hear it."

"But you always seem to know the answers," said Tiny Dragon.

Big Panda grinned.

"Well, I have made a lot more mistakes than you."

Big Panda nodded his head in understanding.

But despite having learnt so much, Tiny Dragon couldn't stop his mind occasionally wandering back to all the things he would never see again.

The less I try to control the world,
the freer I am to watch it play out in all its untamed wonder."

"I have come to realize that it's not always the situation that is making me unhappy, but the way I think about it.

"I still feel some sadness at the loss of my friends,
my home and, of course, my tea set, but I think maybe
I am learning to be more accepting of things."

"It seems that the more I unclench my hand," said Tiny Dragon,
"the more the world seems to place into it."

Tiny Dragon packed up his tea set in a huge leaf, and they picked their way along winding animal trails and over dark, gurgling streams.

"How are you feeling, little one?"
asked Big Panda.

Tiny Dragon thought for a moment.

"You know," said Tiny Dragon,
"I think this is the best tea set I've ever had."

"Why is that?" asked Big Panda.

"Because it's the one I have now."

"What are we celebrating?" asked Big Panda.

"Us . . ." said Tiny Dragon. "It's been a long journey with many challenges and we're both still here – that seems a good reason to me."

After a little digging,
Tiny Dragon found a round pot
and two mismatched, chipped little cups.

"Come on," he said, picking a few choice buds off a bush.

"I recognize these leaves – they make delicious tea.
Let's celebrate."

They seated themselves under the boughs
of an ancient, twisted tree
and Tiny Dragon prepared a small fire.

Then something caught Tiny Dragon's eye.

Half buried in the soil was a jumble of broken pottery.

So the two friends made their way down into the jungle.
It was more beautiful than Tiny Dragon could have imagined.

Colorful birds in varieties he had never seen, huge plants
with flowers he could have bathed in and strange furred beasts
that crept silently through the undergrowth.

Hunger and cold were forgotten as Tiny Dragon sat motionless, soaking in the beauty of what lay before him.

Eventually Big Panda tapped him on the shoulder with a large paw.

"Come," he said.

"Let's head down and find some food and water."

And as they crested the final rise,
Tiny Dragon was lost for words,
for beyond, a broad river snaked its way through
a magnificent forested valley.

"This," said Big Panda,
"is where our journey has been leading us."

"And this," grinned Tiny Dragon,
"is where we will make our new home."

And sure enough, out of the swirling mists
appeared a peak of jagged rock.

Big Panda gathered his strength
and they struggled up the last stretch.

"Look," said Tiny Dragon, "I can see the top."

"We should be on our way," said Big Panda.
"I don't know how much longer we can last out here."

They had no food or water so they braced
themselves against the cold and the wind
and continued toward the summit.

Tiny Dragon awoke early the next morning
and although rain still swept across the mountains,

where he had previously seen hopelessness and defeat,
he now saw opportunity and beauty.

They watched the sun disappear behind the mountains
and as night settled over the land,
Tiny Dragon spoke for the first time in hours.

"Big Panda," he asked. "What is the universe?"

"I like to think it's our friend," said Big Panda.
"If we allow it to be."

Tiny Dragon looked around to see Big Panda,
soaked through but smiling.

"I think I do," he replied.

"You see, don't you?"

Tiny Dragon couldn't remember seeing
anything so captivating.
So pure, perfect and delicate.

And he began to feel that the emptiness inside him
was like a cup waiting to be filled.

Filled with all the wonders the world had to offer.

There was pain, of course,
but there was so much beauty too.

its earthen hues catching the pale sun
as it broke through the clouds.

So delicate.

So beautiful.

The world in a moment.

Time fell away as he watched it turn.

And then he saw it . . .

hanging from a single strand of spider silk.

A leaf . . .

It was catching just a little of the storm's dying breath,

An overhanging rock was creating the smallest
of dry patches and he staggered over to it,
dropped to the ground, and stared out
at the endless gray skies.

He had no idea how long
he had walked for,
but he was so cold and tired
he knew he had to stop.

Tiny Dragon walked through the downpour
with no idea where he was going.

How could he be complete?

Everything that made him who he was
had been taken away.

Tiny Dragon stood up and walked out of the cave and into the storm.

Big Panda knew he had to let him go.

Big Panda took the tiny, wet dragon into his arms and squeezed him tightly.

"That's true," he said, "and yet, somehow, we are complete."

"And I know it's hard to understand right now," said Big Panda, "but the universe has placed us exactly where we need to be."

Tiny Dragon looked up, tears in his eyes.

"But we are hundreds of miles from home, we don't know where we are, and we have nothing."

"I make no difference to anything,"
said Tiny Dragon.

Big Panda smiled at his friend.
"You make all the difference to me."

Big Panda made his way carefully across the sharp, slippery stone and managed to crawl into the cave formed by a cluster of huge boulders.

They sat together and watched the rain, then Big Panda turned to Tiny Dragon.

"You can talk to me, little one, if you want to."

They struggled onward,
but there was no relief.

Just as the last of his strength was failing,
Big Panda spotted something.

"Look, Tiny Dragon,
we can shelter between those rocks."

But Tiny Dragon was silent.

They journeyed for hours
until the forest gave way
to a bare expanse of rock that
rose sharply toward the
mountain's summit.

The rain was relentless,
lashing the stone and cascading
down gullies.

But Tiny Dragon did not speak, he did not feel the rain,
he barely heard Big Panda's voice.

He felt alone and empty
in a world that meant nothing.

Thunder cracked the sky open
and the rain fell in great sheets that
swept across the forest canopy.

"We must press on and find shelter,"
said Big Panda,
"this could continue for hours,
or even days."

The going was hard.

There was often no path to follow, and thick, tangled roots crawled across the forest floor.

Sometimes it was so steep that they had to find another way, as Big Panda's paws slid and slipped in the thick mud.

"Rain is coming," said Big Panda, looking up at a darkening sky.

"We should search for shelter."

Tiny Dragon climbed onto Big Panda's back,
and they began to ascend the mountain.

But Tiny Dragon found little comfort
in Big Panda's words.

His eyes fell to the stream,
but all he could see was the rock.

"If we have to be lost," said Big Panda,
"I am glad it's with you."

Tiny Dragon looked up at
Big Panda and tried to smile,
tried to see the wisdom in his words,
but his heart was heavy.

Inside he felt he had lost everything.

He was utterly empty.

Big Panda offered a reassuring paw –
"We have gone astray, far from our home.

But . . ."

Big Panda pointed to the
stream next to them.

"You see the way the water
travels around the rock,
Tiny Dragon?

The obstacle is there,
but the water is flowing around it,
taking the gentlest path
to its destination.

We can be the same."

"No," squeaked Tiny Dragon.

"It can't be.

We have to go home.
What about the temple,
and my things,
my friends,
and all my favourite
places . . . ?

No.

We can't stay here . . .
we can't . . ."

Tiny Dragon nodded.

"So how far is it back to the temple?" he asked.

"I think I have learned what I needed to,
I will never take my life for granted again!"

Big Panda put a large paw on his friend's shoulder.

"We cannot go home," he said as the last star
disappeared into the dawn light.

"This is a new world, somewhere we have never been,
and somewhere from which we can never return."

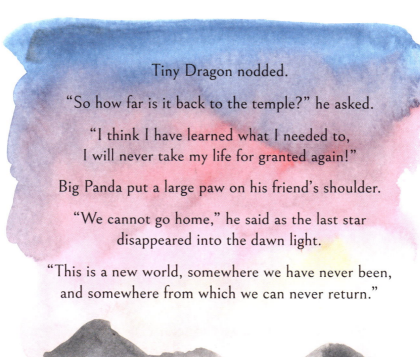

"I never imagined I'd have been so grateful for food and drink,"
said Tiny Dragon, munching on a berry.

"It's funny," said Big Panda,
"how simple things, when seen with fresh eyes,
can often bring the most happiness."

They didn't have to travel long before
they found a patch of thick grass by a winding stream.

Tiny Dragon collected some sweet red berries
and there were even some young shoots of bamboo.

They sat by the water eating, drinking and watching
the sun rise over the ocean.

"Come, little one," said Big Panda.

"Climb on my back and we'll find some food and water."

Tiny Dragon staggered to his feet.

"Big Panda, Big Panda! We're saved."

Big Panda opened his eyes, took in the expanse
of pale sand and the mountains beyond,
and smiled at Tiny Dragon.

Tiny Dragon awoke with a start.

Although it was still dark,
he could see that the raft had become
beached on a sandy shore,
which gleamed white in the moonlight.

Beyond it,
high mountains rose into the night.

Tired and weak, Tiny Dragon fell asleep
and Big Panda looked up at one of
the most beautiful nights he'd ever seen.

"But what if I'm somewhere I don't want to be?"
asked Tiny Dragon.

"That does happen," said Big Panda,
"and of course, we can try to change our
circumstances for the better,

but some situations, like this one, we cannot change
and should try to accept as they are.

That acceptance brings with it great peace."

Big Panda pulled Tiny Dragon in close.
"Nothing is under our control, little one . . . not really.

I just trust in life to take us where we need to be."

Hours stretched into days.

Each morning
the sun rose a burning red
over the mirror-ocean,
but there was no sign of land.

One night, Tiny Dragon,
weak from hunger and thirst,
crawled up to Big Panda
and snuggled into his fur.

"How can you be so calm?"
he asked.

"This could be the end."

And Tiny Dragon tried . . .

But in that stillness,
all he could think of was how he had lost
his treasured tea set, how they had no food
or water and how far from home they were . . .

So he did all he could think of
and started paddling.

"If you feel lost," said Big Panda, "just close your eyes.

Hear the water lapping against the raft,

feel the sun on your skin and the breeze against your face.

There you are.

You will find yourself soon enough."

Tiny Dragon gazed out at the endless ocean stretching away in every direction.

"We have never been this lost," he sighed.

"This is not where we would
choose to be," said Big Panda,

"but it is where we are . . .

And if you try to forget about what has
happened, just for a moment,
and look around,

you might see that this is
one of the most beautiful moments
we have ever experienced."

"Oh no!" exclaimed Tiny Dragon.

"We're going to die!"

"We're safe!" squeaked Tiny Dragon,
and gave Big Panda a huge hug.

"But where are we?
I don't see the banks of the Great River."

"The storm raged all night," said Big Panda.
"We've been swept into the ocean."

Big Panda felt the sun on his back and opened his eyes.

His fur was matted with salt and his body ached, but he was reassured to feel Tiny Dragon's body curled up in his fur.

It wasn't long until his little friend awoke and crawled out into the morning air.

By morning, the storm had blown itself out.

The raft drifted aimlessly on glassy, silent waters.

Even the greatest storm will pass . . .

And Big Panda heard Tiny Dragon's pain.
He wanted to help him and hold him,
and tell him it would be OK.

But he was exhausted and lacked
the strength to speak, and if he loosened
his grip, they would be washed into
the foaming waters.

All he could do was listen and
do his best to keep them safe.

He buried his face in his hands
and sobbed.

What was he doing?
What was the point of all this?

He had never felt like this in his life.

Opening one eye, he could see it lying on the raft, the cloth wrap caught on a sharp piece of wood.

He reached out his hand to grab it, just as the raft banged against a large rock.

The tea set broke free and tumbled into the water.

As he watched it vanish into the black, churning depths he felt as though his heart had followed it.

Tiny Dragon was too scared to talk.

He screwed his eyes closed
and clung on as hard as he could.

But then he suddenly remembered his tea set.

Dark clouds loomed above them
and the rain fell hard and icy,
turning the surface of the river
into a ragged froth.

The raft began to spin and buck,
and the downpour had made
the wood cold, slippery and wet.

It was all Tiny Dragon could do to hold on.

Big Panda laid out flat to make himself
as stable as possible, and with a large paw,
tucked Tiny Dragon into his fur
to keep him warm and safe.

"Aren't you scared of storms?" asked Tiny Dragon.

"Maybe once," said Big Panda, "but I've survived them all – I've learnt that I don't need to be afraid."

But the current was stronger than it looked and despite their efforts, they couldn't steer the boat toward the bank.

Tiny Dragon started to panic, but Big Panda just calmly paddled.

Then from nowhere a deep rumble shook the land, and Tiny Dragon felt spots of rain and a chilling wind.

"A storm is coming," said Big Panda, looking up at the gathering clouds. "We should make for the shore."

Tiny Dragon fell silent and thought about Big Panda's words.

"Surely the past makes a difference?"
said Tiny Dragon.

"You're right," said Big Panda, "the past is like a story that tells us how we arrived where we are – but you can start writing a new story right now."

"This raft is a little like us,"
said Big Panda.

"Where it's been doesn't have
to determine where it's going."

As the sun was starting to set, Big Panda dragged the raft
into the shallows of the river.

They both climbed on board and Tiny Dragon used
his pole to push them off the bank.

They let the current take the raft for a while
and carry them down the river.

"And yet," said Big Panda, "gathering bamboo is not so different from gathering sticks.

Sometimes good and bad are just ways of looking at the world."

By the afternoon they had built a small raft.

It was not much to look at, but it would carry them across the river.

"I enjoyed that," said Tiny Dragon, taking in what they had made.

Despite how he felt inside, Tiny Dragon gave a big smile and puffed out his little chest.

"I'll get the bamboo. You collect the logs."

Together they searched the shoreline until Big Panda found what he was looking for.

"The weather can be fierce here," he said, pointing at some trees that had come down in a storm.

"If we use bamboo to make rope and lash together the trunks, we'll have a raft in no time."

Tiny Dragon finished his berry.
"You're right," he said.

"Crossing the river does scare me –
and so I'll be scared when I do it
– but I'm going to cross it regardless."

Great change requires great effort."

They watched the sun break over dark mountains.

"Something needs to change, my little friend,"
said Big Panda.

"But if making the change was easy,
it probably wouldn't make very much difference.

"It's natural to be scared," said Big Panda,
"but sometimes we must carry on anyway."

"Fear will not stop you dying,
but it may stop you from living."

In the morning, while they were
breakfasting on bamboo and berries,
Big Panda noticed Tiny Dragon
was looking worried.

"What is it, little one?"

Tiny Dragon looked up.

"I'm afraid," he said quietly.
"I don't want to cross the river."

"And if you forget yourself,
just look up at the stars in the sky,
or listen to the pines waving in the evening breeze.

They are doing what nature intended – in this moment."

Tiny Dragon felt that Big Panda was only reminding him of something he already knew deep inside.

"Stillness is always there to be found," said Big Panda.
"And in that peace you may start to find yourself again."

Big Panda thought for a moment.

"Our thoughts can lead us away from ourselves.

When you were young, the task of gathering sticks probably took all your attention.

When you are focused in that way, your mind tends not to wander and that creates a sense of inner stillness from which arise feelings of joy and peace."

Tiny Dragon pondered.

"Perhaps you're right. When I was collecting them just now, I was thinking about whether this journey would really help.

I was not really thinking about the sticks at all."

"I used to love choosing the best sticks, brushing off the leaves and placing them in my basket."

Tiny Dragon poked the fire with a stick.

"Big Panda?

I was wondering . . .

why don't I get the same pleasure collecting sticks now that I did when I was a very tiny dragon?"

"We'll stop here tonight," said Big Panda.
"We can light a fire and listen to the river."

"And I will make some tea!" said Tiny Dragon.

Tiny Dragon collected some sticks and soon water was heating over the crackling fire.

Until one evening,
just as the stars were starting to come out,
they arrived at the banks of the Great River.

They traveled for many days through the dense forests that covered the mountains.

They passed crashing waterfalls and dark, deep pools.

They saw colorful birds and glimpsed small deer flitting through the towering bamboo.

And so Tiny Dragon clambered up onto
Big Panda's back and they followed the rocky trail
that led out of the mountains and down to the river,
leaving the old temple far behind them.

"Of course," said Big Panda.

"There is nothing wrong with enjoying the fruits of the world, we just need to make sure we do not lose ourselves in them."

Tiny Dragon paused – deep down he knew Big Panda was right, but he had one small question.

"Can I take my tea set?"

"Everything you need," said Big Panda,
"is already inside you."

When Big Panda saw the overstuffed cart, he slowly shook his head.

"We cannot take all of this over the river."

"But I need these things," said Tiny Dragon, stroking his picture of Grandpa Dragon.

When he was finished, he placed a
few of his most-prized possessions into his little cart
and went outside to meet Big Panda.

They returned to the temple to close the wooden shutters and block up the broken doorway, for it rained a lot in the mountains and Tiny Dragon did not want his things to get wet while they were away.

They left the garden and walked to the cliff
that overlooked the Great River.

After settling himself on the rock,
Big Panda turned to Tiny Dragon.

"We cannot just sit here and hope the
weeds will go away on their own.

We must take action.

Sometimes something needs to change,
and that requires effort.

We shall go on a journey, across the river."

"I will help you," said Big Panda.

"Remember, little one –
together we can do anything."

Tiny Dragon nodded.

"But how do I pull up the weeds?"

"In some ways, the mind is much like a garden.
It needs your care, attention and effort.

Left to its own devices it will soon become overrun with weeds.
And where there are too many weeds, flowers cannot grow."

They crossed the old bridge that led to the temple's garden.

"Change," said Big Panda, "even if you don't know where it will lead, is better than stagnation."

"I'd help you," said Tiny Dragon,
"if you ever needed it."

"You help me every day," replied Big Panda,
"just by being yourself."

"You have shared how you feel," said Big Panda.

"Sharing our lives, both the good and the bad, is what makes us closer and lets us help each other."

"Problems should not stop us," said Big Panda.

"They are simply nature's way of letting us know we need to explore a different path."

Big Panda awoke early, but his friend
was already up watching the sun
rise over the mountains.

He seated himself on the rock
next to Tiny Dragon.

"You are unhappy, my little friend," said Big Panda.
"That's OK. It happens to us all.

The important thing is that you have
noticed something is wrong."

Big Panda nodded
and took a sip of tea.

"That is a good question, little one,
and the answer is simple yet difficult.

Sleep now.

Tomorrow is a new day,
and we'll see what we can do."

One winter evening, under a full moon,
Tiny Dragon turned to his friend and said,

"This place is incredible, Big Panda.
The trees, the mountains, the birds and the animals,
they are all so magical; we are so lucky –
so why do I feel like something is missing?

Why do I feel incomplete?"

At night they would watch the stars
and drink the hot tea that Tiny Dragon
so carefully prepared.

And explore the thick, tangled forests hoping to catch
a glimpse of the creatures that lived there.

During the day they would travel high into the mountain peaks.

Big Panda and Tiny Dragon.

But that didn't matter
to the two friends
who made that ancient
place their home.

The temple had seen better days.

And a deep, still lake.

Surrounded by a vast forest.

There was a temple high in the mountains.

For those on their own journey.

The Journey

Big Panda and Tiny Dragon

James Norbury

MANDALA

SAN RAFAEL LOS ANGELES LONDON

The Journey